E/
BOO

Eat Like a Local- Sarasota: Sarasota Florida Food Guide

I have lived in the Sarasota area since 1998 and learned about many great places that I want to try. –Conoal

Eat Like a Local: Connecticut: Connecticut Food Guide

This a great guide to try different places in Connecticut to eat. Can't wait to try them all. The author is awesome to explore and try all these different foods/drinks. There are places I didn't know they existed until I got this book and I am a CT resident myself. –Caroline J. H.

Eat Like a Local: Las Vegas: Las Vegas Nevada Food Guide

Perfect food guide for any tourist traveling to Vegas or any local looking to go outside their comfort zone. – TheBondes

Eat Like a Local-Jacksonville: Jacksonville Florida Food Guide

Loved the recommendations. Great book from someone who knows their way around Jacksonville. –Anonymous

Eat Like a Local- Costa Brava: Costa Brava Spain Food Guide

The book was very well written. Visited a few of the restaurants in the book, they were great. Sylvia V.

Eat Like a Local-Sacramento: Sacramento California Food Guide

As a native of Sacramento, Emerald's book touches on some of our areas premier spots for food and fun. She skims the surface of what Sacramento has to offer recommending locations in historical, popular areas where even more jewels can be found. –Katherine G.

EAT LIKE A LOCAL- ROARING FORK VALLEY

*From Glenwood Springs to Aspen
Colorado Food Guide*

Scotty Jeffus

CZYK Publishing Since 2011.
CZYKPublishing.com
Eat Like a Local

Mill Hall, PA
All rights reserved.
ISBN: 9798867446000

BOOK DESCRIPTION

Are you excited about planning your next trip? Do you want an edible experience? Would you like some culinary guidance from a local? If you answered yes to any of these questions, then this Eat Like a Local book is for you. Eat Like a Local – Roaring Fork Valley From Glenwood Springs to Aspen Colorado Food Guide by Scotty Jeffus offers the inside scoop on food in Colorado's Roaring Fork Valley.

Culinary tourism is an important aspect of any travel experience. Food has the ability to tell you a story of a destination, its landscapes, and culture on a single plate. Most food guides tell you how to eat like a tourist. Although there is nothing wrong with that, as part of the Eat Like a Local series, this book will give you a food guide from someone who has lived at your next culinary destination.

In these pages, you will discover advice on having a unique edible experience. This book will not tell you exact addresses or hours but instead will give you excitement and knowledge of food and drinks from a local that you may not find in other travel food guides.

Eat like a local. Slow down, stay in one place, and get to know the food, people, and culture. By the time you finish this book, you will be eager and prepared to travel to your next culinary destination.

OUR STORY

Traveling has always been a passion of the creator of the Eat Like a Local book series. During Lisa's travels in Malta, instead of tasting what the city offered, she ate at a large fast-food chain. However, she realized that her traveling experience would have been more fulfilling if she had experienced the best of local cuisines. Most would agree that food is one of the most important aspects of a culture. Through her travels, Lisa learned how much locals had to share with tourists, especially about food. Lisa created the Eat Like a Local book series to help connect people with locals which she discovered is a topic that locals are very passionate about sharing. So please join me and: Eat, drink, and explore like a local.

TABLE OF CONTENTS

Section 3: Glenwood Springs

13. Small Shack, Big Flavor
14. Way Down Below
15. Glenwood Grinder
16. Taste as Big as Everest
17. Blast from the Past
18. Hot Food, Cool Vibes
19. The Moose's Finest

Section 4: Carbondale

20. The Old Wild West is Alive
21. Valley's Tallest Mushroom
22. A Mountain Full of Liquor
23. A Whole New World
24. Taste of South America
25. Big, Phat Thai
26. When Honey Meets Butter
27. Where's the Beef?

Section 5: El Jebel and Basalt

28. Wide Open Spaces
29. Sunday Fun-day
30. Middle East meets the Rocky Mountains
31. Essen aus den Bergen (Food from the Mountains)
32. Beer Creek

Top Ten

Top 10 drinks in the Roaring Fork Valley.

Top 10 foods to try in the Roaring Fork Valley

Top 10 souvenirs to get in the Roaring Fork Valley

Top 10 must take pictures in the Roaring Fork Valley

Top 10 sites to see in the Roaring Fork Valley

Top_10 culture shocks when visiting the Roaring Fork Valley

Top_10 scams I should look out for when visiting the Roaring Fork Valley?

Other Resources:

Taste of the Seasons

READ OTHER BOOKS BY CZYK PUBLISHING

DEDICATION

I want to dedicate this book to my grandmother, Carol Scott (Nana). She was one of the most incredible home cooks I've ever known, and she is the reason why I fell in love with food.

I would also like to dedicate this book to my father, David Jeffus, who helped introduce me to Glenwood Springs and helped me fall in love with the valley in the first place.

ABOUT THE AUTHOR

Marshall Scott (Scotty) Jeffus is a food writer who lives in the great town of Glenwood Springs, Colorado. He loves food and loves to cook, so much so that he went to Le Cordon Bleu culinary school in Austin, Texas, where he grew up, and graduated with an honor's degree.

However, after seven years of working as a chef in various restaurant kitchens in Texas and Colorado, Scotty decided that the stressful restaurant scene wasn't fit for him, so he put down the knives and picked up the keyboard to become a food content writer for an Italian food/recipe blog called Pastalove.net.

This will be the first book Scotty has ever written, and he could not be more thrilled.

HOW TO USE THIS BOOK

The goal of this book is to help culinary travelers either dream or experience different edible experiences by providing opinions from a local. The author has made suggestions based on their own knowledge. Please do your own research before traveling to the area in case the suggested locations are unavailable.

Travel Advisories: As a first step in planning any trip abroad, check the Travel Advisories for your intended destination.
https://travel.state.gov/content/travel/en/traveladvisories/traveladvisories.html

FROM THE PUBLISHER

Traveling can be one of the most important parts of a person's life. The anticipation and memories that you have are some of the best. As a publisher of the *Eat Like a Local*, Greater Than a Tourist, as well as the popular *50 Things to Know* book series, we strive to help you learn about new places, spark your imagination, and inspire you. Wherever you are and whatever you do I wish you safe, fun, and inspiring travel.

Lisa Rusczyk Ed. D.
CZYK Publishing

"People who love to eat are
always the best people."

- Julia Child
Reference: 75 Best Food Quotes and Captions
from toasttab.com

Colorado's Roaring Fork Valley is the place that I have called home since 2017 and is full of all sorts of different restaurants and sights to see. Whether you're in Glenwood Springs, Aspen, or any neighboring town, you will surely find something delicious to eat.

What I wish to do is share the hidden gems that each of the valley's great towns has to offer and how to get the best experience the next time you decide to visit.

I won't be going over every restaurant and food destination within the valley because…that would make this book at least three times as long, but I will be sharing the best spots I have come across in the five years I have lived there.

Also, I would like to make a quick note that this book won't be all about food entirely. It will be food-centered, no doubt, but there will also be sections that talk about fun activities and attractions that only add to the valley's natural beauty.

Roaring Fork Valley, Colorado
United States

Aspen Colorado Climate

	High	Low
January	36	10
February	39	13
March	46	21
April	53	27
May	63	35
June	74	43
July	79	48
August	76	47
September	70	41
October	58	31
November	45	20
December	35	11

GreaterThanaTourist.com

Temperatures are in Fahrenheit degrees.
Source: NOAA

SECTION 1: THE VALLEY

1. WHAT IS THE ROARING FORK VALLEY?

Colorado's Roaring Fork Valley (RFV) is a geographical region in the mid-western area of Colorado that extends from Glenwood Springs to Independence Pass, about fifty miles.

The valley holds a wide range of small but busy towns, such as Carbondale, Basalt, and Aspen, all of which are full of stunning restaurants and food destinations to choose from. My first tip when traveling through the valley is to go in with an open mind and not be afraid to explore.

2. VALLEY HISTORY

The Roaring Fork Valley was first inhabited by the Ute people, settlers who inhabited Western Colorado's deserts as long as 2000 years ago, and the first to travel over the historic Independence Pass in 1879 to hunt for silver.

13

Aspen blossomed as a mining community in the late 1880s until the silver crash of 1893, but it wasn't long after that coal mining in the Valley of the Crystal began to spread like wildfire, which helped build the valley into what it is today.

The name Roaring Fork comes from a lively mountain stream that starts at Independence Lake, at an elevation of 12,500 feet and runs about 50 miles through the valley until it eventually meets up with the Colorado River in the north area of Glenwood Springs.

3. RAPTOR RIDING

Don't want to take your car up and down the valley? Not to worry, because a quick and energy-efficient way to get around is with the Roaring Fork Transportation Authority (RFTA), which is there to get you where you need to go for a relatively low price. However, if you need to be somewhere at a specific time, I suggest some extra planning by figuring out where the nearest stop is and researching the bus schedule.

4. DRINK RESPONSIBLY

One of the best exports from Colorado is the wide array of craft beer, whiskey, and tequila that hit the bars and restaurants all over the state every day.

While the occasional drink is more than acceptable, like after a stressful day of working, you need to remember that at high altitudes, alcohol tends to travel through your body quicker, and you end up feeling intoxicated faster. You are free to live your life as you wish, but I strongly suggest that you do so responsibly.

5. FARM TO MARKET TO PLATE

Throughout the summertime, when you're not splashing in the Colorado River on a whitewater raft or hiking up to one of the many great lakes studded throughout the valley, a fantastic place that you must visit would be the wonderful farmer's markets that go on all throughout the summer where local growers, vendors, and artists come together and show the valley what they do best.

What you need to understand is that not every market will have the exact same produce or products week after week, town after town, and they do sell out quickly, so you will want to get to each market as soon as you can to ensure that you get exactly what you're looking for.

Also, don't be afraid to be adventurous and try something new while you're there, like an Argentinian-style sausage sandwich, freeze-dried Skittles candy, or even try on some of the locally made jewelry.

SECTION 2: COLORADO CUISINE

6. WHERE THE DEER AND THE WAPITI PLAY

I could not make a book all about the great Colorado valley that I live in without talking about some of my favorite parts of the local cuisine that fills the hearts and stomachs of Coloradans from Denver to Grand Junction.

If you're an adventurous eater like me, then you may find yourself diving into a local Colorado delicacy that roams the mountains like no other: elk.

Elk has a bit of a grassy, meaty flavor as well as the protein content of beef with half the fat, and certain restaurants all over Colorado serve it; one of my favorite ways to eat it happens to be an elk burger with goat's cheese, blueberry sauce, and roasted poblano peppers from a restaurant that I used to work at, The Tipsy Trout in Basalt.

7. TASTE THE RAINBOW

Not adventurous enough to try elk? Not to worry, because swimming in the stunning lakes and rivers all around RFV, and all of Colorado for that matter, happens to be another local favorite, freshwater trout, which has a light, delicate flavor and firm flesh that makes it a valley staple.

There are at least a hundred different ways to cook and eat trout, but my favorite goes like this: Lightly grilled whole rainbow trout stuffed with lemon and capers, then served amandine style with green beans, potatoes, almonds, and a light butter sauce.

8. SILENCE OF THE LAMB

Lamb might as well be the new red meat as many restaurants and grocery stores, especially in Colorado, now provide this tasty meat in the form of lamb chops, burgers, and legs of lamb that are roasted for the holidays.

Lamb can be cooked in about as many ways as beef, maybe a few more, but one of my favorites has to be a classic herb-crusted rack of lamb served with chimichurri.

The thing to remember about lamb is that the longer it cooks, the tougher it can become, so if you're not a fan of medium-rare meat, then I'm afraid you're out of luck there.

9. A PEACH A DAY KEEPS THE SADNESS AWAY

There is one crop found in RFV that takes the Farmer's market shelves by storm during the summertime: the amazing peaches grown in the small town of Palisade, Colorado, located near Grand Junction.

Sweet, floral, and soft, these golden nuggets of joy are in such high demand that the peach orchards of Palisade can barely stay supplied without an entire valley to feed from late July through mid-October.

When shopping for these beauties, you'll want to look for a few things: Aroma, size (the bigger, the better, as the larger peaches have a higher sugar concentration), and ripeness, which can vary depending on how soon you plan on eating those peaches, although it's not like they're going to last very long.

SECTION 3: GLENWOOD SPRINGS

13. SMALL SHACK, BIG FLAVOR

Among the many great restaurants that call Glenwood Springs home, there exists one on 7th Street that may seem like a small shack from the outside, but within lies some of the best tacos and hot dogs in the state, and that is Slope & Hatch.

Recognized by TripAdvisor as one of the top fifty best tacos in Colorado, Slope and Hatch is a small 20-seat restaurant, but somehow they know how to pack big, bold flavors into their tacos and dogs, such as their jerk chicken tacos with pineapple salsa and mint-coconut crema.

If you're going there with your family, then I would advise getting a variety of tacos and one or two hot dogs so you can experience a wider range of what Slope and Hatch has to offer.

14. WAY DOWN BELOW

When you hear the words 'underground business,' you may think of something like a shady organization, but what if I told you that a well-established Italian restaurant is tucked underneath the streets of Glenwood?

The Italian Underground, fittingly located under the Grand Avenue bridge, is a small restaurant found under a women's clothing store, Elizabeth Dean Boutique, that serves up tasty, scratch-made pizza and spaghetti that take the town of Glenwood by storm.

My only tips for going to this hidden wonder is this: Get there as early as you can; although The Italian Underground is only open for dinner, they don't take reservations and can fill up very quickly, and while their pizza is quite popular, I personally found myself enjoying their spaghetti and pasta dishes a lot more.

15. GLENWOOD GRINDER

Would you believe me if I told you that sitting between the incredible tacos and hot dogs from Slope & Hatch and the Italian Underground lies one of the best hamburger restaurants in RFV?

The Grind on 7th Street is a hip spot featuring hamburgers made with grass-fed beef and a full bar of craft beer that locals and tourists of Glenwood Springs can't seem to get enough of, and the French fries keep on coming.

While their beef burgers are iconic, I find myself going for their Mediterranean-style Colorado lamb burger, which features marinated tomatoes, feta cheese, and tzatziki sauce.

16. TASTE AS BIG AS EVEREST

When driving through Glenwood Springs along the historic I-70 highway, you might not believe that, in this smallish Colorado mountain town, you'll find authentic Indian cuisine.

Located in Glenwood Meadows, a shopping district in East Glenwood, Everest Nepal Restaurant, and its sister location found between Glenwood and Carbondale, is an Indian-style restaurant/buffet that brings the rich, spicy, flavorful cuisine for locals to dive into.

While you could certainly order some a la carte dishes, Everest's buffet offers you a wider variety of authentic Indian fare for a fraction of the price, so you might cnd up trying one or two new items you may like, such as tandoori chicken, saag paneer (spinach and cheese dish) or some of their house-made naan bread.

17. BLAST FROM THE PAST

Do you remember the fifties when you would go to a drive-in restaurant for cheap hamburgers, French fries, and shakes and have a wholesome, simple outing with friends or family?

Well, I wasn't around yet, but if you wish to return, Vicco's Charcaolburger off Highway 6 is the right place for you.

Since 1953, Vicco's burger drive-in has become a staple in the hearts of Glenwood Springs residents with their 1/3 pound all-beef burger patties cooked to flavorful perfection and cooked to order, so you know you're getting a fresh, juicy, delicious burger every time.

18. HOT FOOD, COOL VIBES

Keeping with the '50s theme, we now head down Glenwood's Grand Avenue to a pink-roofed diner that provides scratch-made diner food that locals gobble up like it's their last meal, a place that any RFV resident reading this is likely drooling over just thinking about, I speak of the 19th Street Diner.

Breakfast, lunch, or dinner, there is no meal that the 19th Street Diner can't cook up with that warm, comforting feeling of being at home and having a loved one cook for you.

While there is no particular item from the diner's menu that I wouldn't recommend, I do suggest visiting during the weekends, where you can get the king of brunch dishes, Eggs Benedict.

19. THE MOOSE'S FINEST

I've already talked too much about the wonders of Glenwood Springs, but I promise you that this will be the last of it before I move on to Carbondale; besides I could not give a proper tour of Glenwood without ending with something sweet.

If you're a fellow Chocaholic like me, then you need to hear about a shop tucked right at the edge of Bethel Plaza under the Grand Avenue bridge that rolls out quality chocolates and churns up house-made ice cream and that is Chocolate Moose and Ice Cream Parlor.

Whether you need to get your chocolate fix, are looking to cool off with a tasty treat, or wish to treat yourself to sugary perfection, Chocolate Moose has something that will hit the spot every time, and if you're going after their chocolates then try getting an assortment so you can try an array of different flavors and textures.

SECTION 4: CARBONDALE

20. THE OLD WILD WEST IS ALIVE

Located towards the base of the huge and stunning Mt. Sopris, Carbondale might seem like an unsuspecting small mountain town, but much like Glenwood Springs, it is full of huge personalities and lots of fun, and during the summer months, many Carbondale residents turn to a wild pastime that is older than the town itself.

Held every Thursday from the first week of June to the last week of August, The Carbondale Wild West Rodeo takes in ranchers from all over the valley, and they show off their stuff with lassoing, bull riding, and much more.

If I had to give any advice to those interested in the wild show, it would be to get there as early as possible, as the seats fill up quickly, and try going with someone who knows a thing or two about the rodeo so you won't get too confused.

21. VALLEY'S TALLEST MUSHROOM

Hiking is a very popular pastime in the Roaring Fork Valley, which should not be a surprise considering the dense forests, stunning lakes, and striking views that the mountains of Colorado are famed for, and right above the North end of Carbondale sits the widely popular Mushroom Rock trail.

With 1.5 miles of unique rock formations, blue bushes, and trees that seem to stretch into the sky, Mushroom Rock takes roughly 1 ½ hours to complete, but any hiking lover can tell you that it's well worth the time.

As with hiking in general, the best tips I can give you are to stay hydrated as much as possible, stay on the trail, and don't forget to stop for a moment to take in the views that make up the valley's beauty.

22. A MOUNTAIN FULL OF LIQUOR

I'm not a huge drinker, although I do enjoy a cocktail, beer, or a glass of wine with dinner now and then, but I do believe it's important to have a reliable source for drinks that also has a wide variety, and for that, I often turn to Sopris Liquor and Wine in Carbondale for just that.

You name a spirit, wine, or beer, and Sopris likely has it in stock; there have been more than one occasion where I wanted to make a cocktail with a specific type of liquor, and I was able to find it there.

When you do go to Sopris, try going in with an open mind and maybe buying a type of wine or beer that you've never had before and see if you like it; like many liquor stores, they also have small liquor bottles so you can sample something you haven't tasted yet to see if it would be worth buying a full bottle.

23. A WHOLE NEW WORLD

About 30 miles south of Carbondale, located to the East of the small town of Marble, there lies the breathtaking Beaver Lake, a sizeable swimmable lake that feels like a completely different world with its crystal-clear water, lush forests, and the occasional elk, but do be mindful of any paddle-boarders or kayakers that might be taking advantage of the lake's beauty as well.

Sure, this lake isn't in Carbondale, necessarily, but with its cool fresh water, surrounding mountains, and a few trout here and there, Beaver Lake is a hidden Roaring Fork Valley gem that I could not recommend visiting enough.

While heading over there, make sure to stop by the equally stunning Hayes Creek Falls, which will blow your mind with its natural beauty, more on that later.

24. TASTE OF SOUTH AMERICA

I have already talked about the wonders of the RFV farmer's markets that pop up throughout the summertime, but I felt the need to make a shoutout to something that I find myself almost addicted to, and that is the wonderful Argentinian-style sandwiches, or choripan, from Domingo Sausage Co.

Domingo is a family-owned catering company that has sausages running through their DNA and have a passion for sharing that love with RFV with their pop-up tents at the Farmer's Markets in Aspen, Carbondale, and Basalt.

While their sausages pack loads of flavor, I always find myself sinking my teeth into their grilled pork sausage known as bondio, which is topped with provolone cheese and their house-made chimichurri sauce for a perfect bite.

25. BIG, PHAT THAI

Over the years, I have grown a strong fondness for Thai food and the rainbow of flavors that this Southeast Asian country provides, so when I heard that there's a restaurant in Carbondale that provides modern Thai cuisine, I knew I had to check it out.

Sitting on Carbondale's Main Street, Phat Thai has never claimed to be an authentic Thai restaurant, in fact, the owners, Eric Mitchell and Chef Mark Fischer, aren't even Thai, but what they do is take their love and passion for the herbs, peanuts, and chilis that are part of what makes Thai food what we know it to be and gave it a unique twist with big, bold flavors and techniques that makes it one of the most unique restaurants in the valley.

My only tip, and this is something that the owners of Phat Thai will tell you as well, is don't go in expecting the exact same flavors or dishes that you'd expect in a traditional Thai restaurant but keep an open mind, and I'm sure you'll love it.

26. WHEN HONEY MEETS BUTTER

While I can't say enough good things about the 19th Street Diner in Glenwood Springs, there is another diner near the entrance to Carbondale off Highway 82 that also knows how to serve up juicy, crispy fried chicken and signature milkshakes that RFV residents can't get enough of.

A Carbondale icon for decades, Honey Butter Diner, previously known as Red Rock Diner before being bought by the Slow Grovin' family, is no stranger to serving buttermilk-brined, battered chicken fried to golden, crispy perfection and served with their sweet, sticky hot honey.

Now, if you ask for your chicken to be 'dipped' then it will come to you glistening with that hot, sticky goodness, and the only thing that could possibly wash it all down would have to be one of their next-level milkshakes, like their salted caramel-pretzel shake.

27. WHERE'S THE BEEF?

Right here in the Roaring Fork Valley, of course, as there are dozens of steakhouses studded throughout Colorado, and if locally sourced steaks on a comfortable patio with a well-stocked bar sounds like your kind of place, then Carbondale's Brass Anvil has what you need.

The food at Brass Anvil might claim to be modest, but I say that's an understatement for the massive amount of flavor, texture, and aroma each of their stunning dishes offers, like their grilled double-cut pork chop that's glazed with Carolina mustard sauce and served with local squash puree and Palisade fruit reduction.

While the steaks at Brass Anvil are the closest thing to being from another world as we can get, if you're looking to save a few bucks, then they do have a tasty, reasonably priced lunch menu that is as unique as it is flavorful.

SECTION 5: EL JEBEL AND BASALT

28. WIDE OPEN SPACES

During the sunny summer days in Colorado, we all need a place where we can stretch our legs, run around, and get some energy out of ourselves and our kids' systems, and there are few places El Jebel and Basalt residents turn to more than Crown Mountain Park.

With over 120 acres to explore, Crown Mountain Park allows you to get in touch with the outdoors with a wide playground area, exercise equipment, and bike trail to allow you to fill your lungs with fresh mountain air and have a bit of fun while you do so.

Hearing this, you may be inclined to bring your dog to the park so it can get some exercise as well, like I sometimes do for my little dog, Ziggy, but do keep a close eye on your canine companion as there aren't any actual gates separating the park from the nearby street or parking lot.

29. SUNDAY FUN-DAY

I've already talked about the amazing farmer's markets that are studded throughout RFV during the summertime, but I feel like I can't say enough good things about the Basalt Sunday Market held every Sunday from June to September near Lions Park.

There are a lot of great booths and stands that make the Basalt market feel like you're walking into another world, such as the locally crafted wine from Peony Lane, locally grown produce from Barajas Dream Orchard, and if you're lucky, you might find yourself sinking your teeth into some wood-fired pizza from Dustino's Pizza.

If you're buying produce for yourself, I suggest keeping some cash with you as using a credit card for about $2 worth of produce might feel a little awkward, and don't be afraid to ask to sample some of the goods they supply.

30. MIDDLE EAST MEETS THE ROCKY MOUNTAINS

When driving through the small, charming town of El Jebel, you'd likely expect to find comforting food that your mother likely cooked for you growing up, but I doubt you'd expect to find Middle Eastern cuisine.

Jaffa is a small Middle Eastern restaurant/bakery located in a strip mall next to City Market that serves up a wide range of classic desert dishes such as hummus, kababs, and a spicy merguez sandwich, all of which are loaded with herbs, olive oil and tahini that makes that kind of food so delicious.

However, even more impressive is the wide array of pastries and baked goods that they sell, with Middle Eastern classics like baklava and a few French classics like macarons and croissants, the possibilities are endless.

31. ESSEN AUS DEN BERGEN (FOOD FROM THE MOUNTAINS)

As if Middle Eastern food wasn't enough of a surprise, El Jebel is also home to Wienerstube, a German restaurant on Market Street that brings the culinary delights of the Alps to this small Coloradan town with German classics like soft pretzels with mustard, schnitzel, and even an inspired burger with Swiss cheese, elk bratwurst, and a homemade goat's cheese spread.

German food might not seem familiar to all, but the truth is that many American folks are already eating foods that take German inspiration.

Those giant pretzels you get at ballparks are German-inspired, hot dogs are essentially a cheap but tasty variation on Vienna sausages, Vienna being the capital of Austria but that sits right under Germany, and pickles happen to be very similar to some of the delicious German fermented products like sauerkraut or red cabbage, so there's no reason to be afraid of the cuisine of the Alps.

32. BEER CREEK

If there is one beverage Coloradans know how to make, it's beer, in fact there are more breweries in Colorado than in most other states.

I'm not going to sit here and list all of the best breweries and beers that the state has to offer as I don't wish to be here all day, but I will tell you about a place to get bubbly, tasty beers and just-as tasty food to go with it, and that is El Jebel's Capitol Creek Brewery, located right next to Wienerstube on Market Street.

With over a dozen house-made beers on a seasonally changing brew list, you are guaranteed to find a beer to enjoy sipping on while you watch the game or hang out with your buddies, as for the food, my recommendation would have to be any one of their stacked sandwiches with their ultra-crispy home fries on the side.

33. NEED A BURGER? SURE THING.

While The Grind in Glenwood Springs sure knows how to flip their patties, and Vicco's Charcaolburger can transport your tastebuds back to the 1950s, over in El Jebel, there is a place that takes the concept of fast American burgers and flips it on its head: Sure Thing Burger.

Whether it's beef, turkey, or veggie, no burger goes onto Sure Thing's grill that doesn't come out as juicy perfection, and you can load them with as many toppings as your heart desires.

If a place like Sure Thing Burger sounds like your kind of spot, then I suggest getting there as soon as possible as the lines fill up in an instant, and don't forget to try one of their house-blended milkshakes if you have a sweet tooth like me.

34. STONE HORSE

Before moving to Glenwood Springs and while I was still living in Austin, Texas, I would frequently travel up to the mountains to visit my father, David Jeffus, and take in the valley's beauty, and one spot that we always made sure to stop by whenever I visited was the Brick Pony Pub on Basalt's Midland Avenue, and there's no reason why anyone shouldn't.

Brick Pony has a rusty, cozy atmosphere with wonderful drinks and delicious food to back it up, and is a fantastic place to get together with friends for a fun night out.

With classic bar fare like fried pickles, chicken wings, and tacos, there is bound to be something for everyone at The Brick Pony, I recommend their buffalo meatloaf.

35. SHAMELESS WHISKEY

Anyone who has seen Shameless likely knows about the comedically rugged star William H. Macey, but I'll bet you didn't realize that he is the co-owner of a local El Jebel distillery, Woody Creek Distillers.

On top of the celebrity endorsement, Woody Creek Distillers pride themselves on using ingredients from local Colorado farms, such as the rye in their 100% rye mash whiskey or the Rio Grande potatoes for their premium vodka.

While Woody Creek no doubt has a fine selection of gin, vodka, and whiskey that hit the shelves of liquor stores all over the Roaring Fork Valley, I find myself attracted to their straight bourbon, with notes of dark chocolate, honey, and fall spices, a taste that should be enjoyed responsibly.

SECTION 6: ASPEN HIGHLANDS, ASPEN SNOWMASS, AND BUTTERMILK

36. ALPINE SLOPES

I wouldn't call myself an advanced skier, I can barely do anything harder than blue runs, but I have skied in many towns in Colorado, and of all of them, my favorite mountain of all time has to be Snowmass Mountain.

Whether you're a beginner slope shredder, wishing to hit up some jumps and obstacles, or wish to get out there for a fun winter sport, Snowmass has something for you; with 98 trails to choose from that range from green beginner slopes to expert-level double black diamond slopes, there are few skiers or snowboarders who wouldn't feel at home in Snowmass.

Now, the lines for the chairlifts do fill up quickly, especially during the holiday season and spring break, so I would suggest staying towards the mid-section of the mountain with lifts like Big Burn and Alpine Springs, they're further from the crowds, and they all offer a good range of ski trails.

37. HIGHEST LANDS AND THE LOWEST SLOPES

As great of a ski mountain as Snowmass is, I can't forget to mention two of the other mountains that make up the great Aspen ski range, Aspen Highlands, and Buttermilk, both of which offer their own unique range of ski trails.

If you're an intermediate or experienced skier, then Highlands is the right place for you, as the steep mountain makes way for some advanced ski trails that pro skiers line up for.

However, if you're not as experienced with skiing or snowboarding, then the flatter Buttermilk is likely what calls you as it has easier runs that can still be quite fun; Buttermilk is also where the Winter X Games are held, by the way.

38. JINGLE BELLS, MAROON BELLS, JINGLE ALL THE WAY

While the Mushroom Rock hiking trail in Carbondale certainly has its perks, I can't forget to mention one of the most famous hiking trails that RFV has to offer, the iconic Maroon Bells.

The trailhead located a few miles South of Highlands, the Maroon Bells isn't for hiking novices, but it does reward you with some of the most stunning water features that no man could possibly touch, such as the Maroon Lake, Maroon Creek, and Crater Lake.

During peak summer season, the parking lot for Maroon Bells fills up in an instant, so your best bet would be to park in the Basecamp Parking lot in Highlands Village and take a quick shuttle bus up to the trailhead.

39. MOUNTAIN HIGH ALE

Ok, maybe the complex ski slopes of Aspen Highlands aren't for you, that's alright because instead, you could check out a Highlands bar that has been recognized by a certain spiky-haired guy who drives a bright red car, Highlands Alehouse.

Located in the Highlands base village right in front of the Exhibition and Thunderbowl chairlifts, Highlands Alehouse is the perfect spot to relax with a hot meal and cold ales after a long, fun day of shredding the slopes, with a bar menu that features 16 beers on tap, 75 whiskies, and their take on classic bar & grill food.

Whether it's their barbecue chicken pizza, Tuscan chicken panini, or even a classic like a juicy grilled burger, Highlands Alehouse is the right place for good food and cool vibes.

40. ALPINE CUE

Barbecue is an American phenomenon that people drive from all over the country to taste and experience, but I'm here to tell you about a fantastic barbecue restaurant within walking distance from a chairlift.

Home Team BBQ is in The Inn at Aspen near the Aspen airport and at the base of Buttermilk Ski Mountain and is no stranger when it comes to cranking out tender, juicy, smoky meat and flavorful sides that make my mouth water just thinking about it.

While Home Team does have a variety of sauces to choose from, such as their classic red sauce or their hot red, the part of me that grew up in Texas recommends that you taste the meat before adding any additional sauce so you can appreciate the meat's natural flavors.

41. SWISS SUGAR RUSH

If you've ever driven or taken the RFTA bus to or from Aspen to one of the other great towns that make up the valley, then it's very likely that you've driven right past a Swiss bakery that is a tried and true favorite among Aspen residents.

Louis Swiss Bakery is Aspen's oldest full-scale bakery and is still cranking out house-made baked goods to this day; with favorites like artisanal bread, cookies, bagels, and everything in between, there is no pastry that Louis sells that isn't a bite of sweet heaven.

One of my favorite items from Louis has to be their flaky almond croissants, although you may want to load up on some extra napkins as they are quite crumbly and flaky, as a good croissant should be.

42. STIR THE POT

During the long, cold winter months that the Colorado mountains experience, many of us look to a hot bowl of soup to warm us up and deliver a taste that reminds us of home, and whenever I visit Snowmass, there are fewer places I look to for just that than The Stew Pot.

Tucked within the village and about a 5 minute walk from the ski slopes of Snowmass, The Stew Pot has become a favorite among RFV residents with their 50 years of experience ladling out hot, scratch-made soups, stews, and sandwiches for a highly comforting, heart warming bite.

Some of my personal favorites from The Stew Pot would have to be their classic chicken noodle soup or their hot pastrami sandwich, although there is nothing on their menu that I wouldn't recommend trying.

43. BELGIAN BREWS

If you find yourself in Snowmass and need a place to unwind with some craft beer and possibly a bite or two, then you need to kick off your skis and walk over to New Belgium Ranger Station.

The Ranger Station is a local Snowmass favorite and has skiers from all over the valley slide in to dust the snow off their boots and fill their systems with some great food and tasty drinks.

The best time to visit Ranger Station would have to be in the morning on sunny winter days as the small picnic tables can fill up in a flash, but once you get there, you will soon understand how such a small restaurant can be seen as an RFV icon.

44. DELICIOSO DELICIOSO

For this final entry before we head into Aspen, I have decided to talk about Venga Venga, a Mexican restaurant located at the top of the 12-car Skittles gondola in Snowmass that puts their spin on authentic Mexican food for Snowmass visitors and locals to devour.

Venga translates from Spanish to come, which makes sense as Chef Richard Sandoval wants you to come on in and experience the delicious food that Chef Sandoval and his team cook up as if they've been around since Mexico was declared as an official country.

Whether you're looking for something authentic like chicken tacos or their signature classics like grilled quesadillas or even to stop in for some tequila, Venga Venga, like any local restaurant in Snowmass, is the perfect spot for you.

SECTION 7: ASPEN

45. TOO GOOD TO PASS UP

There is no way that I'm going to write a whole book about the Roaring Fork Valley without talking about the stunning mountain pass where it all began, Independence Pass.

Originally known as Hunter Pass, Independence Pass is a driving pass that takes you almost 12,100 feet up to the Continental Divide in the Sawatch mountain range and gives you some of the most breathtaking views of RFV.

To get to the pass, you will need to head Southeast from Aspen and take a narrow, winding mountain road that isn't super rocky, but is not for faint-of-heart drivers, but I promise you that once you get up to the Continental Divide and see the world that surrounds it, you will be glad you did.

46. MOUNTAIN OF LEGENDS

Of the four mountains in and near, Aspen is the only one of those mountains that I have not skied on. However, I can tell you that, with its iconic Silver Queen Gondola, variety of trails, and open atmosphere, Aspen Mountain is worth visiting if you are an avid skier or snowboarder.

Now, the ski trails on Aspen are on the intermediate-advanced side; there are only blue square and black diamond runs, so if you are new to skiing or don't have the confidence to go on the harder runs, then perhaps Snowmass or Buttermilk Mountain are more your speed.

47. HIGH QUALITY, FAIR PRICE

Visiting Aspen and the surrounding mountains can seem like it would cost an arm and a leg just for one night, but what if I told you there's a way to get high-quality food for a fraction of the price?

Once a month during the summertime, the Limelight hotels in Aspen and Snowmass team up with a local brewery, vineyard, or distillery to bring us an incredible 4-course meal with drink pairings that only cost about $60-$65, with the sort of food quality that you could get for a few hundred dollars at other restaurants without even talking about the drinks.

If that kind of thing piques your interest, then I suggest trying to go with a friend, although I can tell you that going alone isn't the worst thing in the world, and if you are a bit of a picky eater or know someone who is that way, then this might not be for you as these are the sorts of dinners that a more adventurous eater like me would like.

48. D'ANGELO FANTASTICO

Almost all my life, I have had a strong love and appreciation for the art of Italian cuisine, so much so that it led to me creating an Italian food blog, so you can bet that if there's a restaurant in Aspen that's serving up their take on modern Italian cuisine, then I was bound to check it out.

Casa D'Angelo is found near the intersection of South Main Street and East Main Street, and its eclectic atmosphere, luscious patio, and chefs that celebrate traditional Italian cuisine with a modern twist make it a restaurant that is more than worth visiting; it's where I celebrated my 27th birthday.

With dishes like their crispy suckling pig, mushroom and black truffle risotto, and grilled organic veal chop, you are guaranteed a treat when visiting Casa D'Angelo.

49. CASA DE CHOLA

The unfortunate truth is that the further you get from our neighbors to the South, the harder it can be to find great-tasting Mexican food, which is why I am proud to present a local restaurant in Aspen that knows how to smash their avocados, pour their tequila, and grill their carne asada for valley locals and visitors to enjoy.

Mi Chola on East Main Street takes the name from the Spanish term for 'My Baby' as, to the co-owners Darren Chapple and Adam Malmgren, the restaurant is their collective gift to Aspen that they care for and ensure that every guest that walks in feels as much love for the restaurant as they do.

Anyone visiting from Texas might be going in and expecting a classic queso dip, that being a bowl of hot, melted cheese that is meant for dipping your chips into, but at Mi Chola, they do a different style of queso called Queso Fundito, which is a lot more stringy and is made with white cheeses and chorizo, but still just as delicious.

50. RED FOX'S LOOT

Frozen yogurt is a tasty trend that serves as a nice, lighter alternative to ice cream, and while you can find self-serve frozen yogurt shops all over the country, over in Aspen, there is a small stand that sells delicious yogurt that you cannot pass up, and that is Red Fox Frozen Yogurt.

With three different flavors of yogurt, a regularly changing sorbet, and as many toppings as you desire, there is hardly a better place to cool down in Aspen than at Red Fox.

One thing to keep in mind is that, like most self-serve frozen yogurt places, Red Fox does charge you by the ounce, so be mindful of this before you think of loading your bowl to the brim.

No matter what town you go to, what restaurants you visit, or what sights you came to see, the Roaring Fork Valley has something for everyone. So, the next time you consider traveling through Western Colorado, make sure to give Glenwood, Aspen, or any of the other wonderful towns in the valley a visit; we will greet you with open arms.

However, if you're still not convinced, then perhaps you should read through these top 10 lists that I have drafted up for you as well.

TOP 10 DRINKS IN THE ROARING FORK VALLEY (IN NO PARTICULAR ORDER)

1. **Razz Beer-Glenwood Canyon Brewpub, Glenwood Springs.**

   Part of a rotating list of seasonal beers at the Brewpub on 7th Street, this fizzy, fruity brew serves as a nice pick-me-up after a long day of working but won't blow away your taste buds like darker beers tend to.

2. **Hanging Lake Light Lager-Glenwood Canyon Brewpub, Glenwood Springs**

   Staying at the Brewpub because there isn't just one great beer that they brew up that fills up the bloodstreams of valley locals, this year-round lager offers a crisp, light flavor that pairs well with any of the food that they serve, especially their appetizers and bar snacks.

3. **Classic Margharita-Frida Mexican Restaurant, Glenwood Springs**

It is hard to go wrong with a great margarita, and while you can get the iconic tequila cocktail anywhere in the valley, Frida's is made with extra love and served in an extra-wide glass that is perfect for sipping while you're having some authentic Mexican food with your friends or family.

4. White Peach Basil Mojito, Ming's Café-Glenwood Springs or Carbondale

I don't think anyone would expect to find a great mojito at an Asian restaurant, but with Mings' unique spin on the classic with aromatic Thai basil and a house-made white peach puree that delivers a punch of sweet-tartness, it might as well be an RFV staple.

5. Yo Bro. Porter-Carbondale Beer Works, Carbondale

I'll admit that I'm not typically a fan of darker beer like Porters, I normally prefer lighter stuff like ales, lagers, and the occasional IPA, but the

Yo Bro. Porter over at Carbondale Beer Works does have a nice dark richness that pairs well with chocolate and red meat.

6. **Passion Fruit Pale Ale, Capitol Creek Brewery-El Jeb**

Once again, we find ourselves with another fruity beer, something that I find myself quite fond of, as the tart flavor of the passion fruit blended with the mild hop flavor from the beer makes it a great socializing beer.

7. **Breck Agave Wheat Beer-Base Camp Bar & Grill**

Base Camp Bar & Grill at the base of Snowmass Mountain is a top pick for great food, a charming atmosphere, and the occasional sound of live music, and their Breck Agave Wheat beer provides a hint of agave sweetness with a nice light flavor.

8. **90-proof straight bourbon-Woody Creek Distillers**

I already talked about this whiskey in my section about Woody Creek Distillers (#35), however, I can't say enough great things about their straight bourbon.

The Woody Creek straight bourbon features a blend of 70% corn, 15% rye, and 15% malted barley (all of which is locally grown) that is aged for at least 5 years for a bourbon that would make the state of Kentucky get down on its knees.

9. Independence Pass IPA-Aspen Brewing Company

IPA beers aren't necessarily for novice beer drinkers, the bitter, hoppy flavors can be rather intense, however, the Independence Pass IPA that the Aspen Brewing Company serves up does provide those same bitter notes with a citrusy, floral flavor to back it up.

10. Japanese-style rice lager-Upslope Brewing Company

Coming in from a brewing company based in Boulder, this unique Japanese lager is a beer that has flaked rice added to the brew to give it a light, crisp flavor. Unfortunately, this does not make the Japanese lager a gluten-free beer; it is still brewed with wheat, but its delicate flavor makes it a perfect pairing to a wide range of food.

This lager, and other beers from Upslope, can be found in most liquor stores in the valley.

TOP 10 FOODS TO TRY IN THE ROARING FORK VALLEY

1. Calamari tacos-Slope and Hatch, Glenwood Springs

I've already mentioned how amazing the tacos are at Slope and Hatch on Glenwood's 7th Street, but just mentioning them once cannot possibly be enough.

S&H's unique calamari tacos feature lightly breaded and fried calamari that is tossed with a sweet, sticky chili glaze and then topped with citrus slaw and some black sesame seeds for a light but powerful punch of flavor that might make you forget you are eating squid.

If you're still uncomfortable with the thought of eating squid, then perhaps their tender, shredded beef barbacoa tacos are what you're looking for.

2. Bavarian Pretzel-Glenwood Canyon Brewpub, Glenwood Springs

I do not want to meet someone who says that they do not like a soft, yeasty, salted Bavarian pretzel that, next to the hot dog, is one of mustard's best friends.

The Bavarian pretzel at the Glenwood Canyon Brewpub not only hits all those notes but takes it one step further by pairing the loop of golden delight with a house-made beer-cheese sauce that makes it a perfect snack while you're sipping on one of their many beers.

If you are one of the few folks who doesn't like soft pretzels, then perhaps their spicy but delicious fried cheese curds with barbecue ranch sauce are more of your style.

3. Grilled Pork Sandwich-Domingo Sausage CO at Farmer's Markets in Carbondale and Basalt (summer only)

Yes, I've already mentioned how amazing the Bondio pork sandwich from Domingo Sausage CO. is, but I can't leave it alone.

With the tender, juicy grilled pork steak topped with provolone cheese and bright and acidic chimichurri, all encased in the soft, crusty bread, it is a sandwich that I see myself devouring at least once a week during the summertime. The sad part is that at some point, the summer ends and I end up waiting for that sandwich all over again, but I can assure you that your patience will be rewarded.

4.   Over the top Milkshakes-Honey Butter, Carbondale

While the fried chicken at Honey Butter diner at the north end of Carbondale is nothing short of perfection, there is something that the small diner mixes up that is always worth saving room for, and that is the extravagant milkshakes that might as well be your second meal.

Sure, you can go for a classic vanilla or chocolate shake, however, I do strongly suggest giving one of their out-of-the-box shakes a try, such as their peanut butter boogie shake, which features vanilla ice cream topped with peanut butter and caramel, then topped with chopped Resse's cups and whipped cream.

Or, if you're not a fan of peanut butter, then perhaps their Nutella-banana shake is more of your style, although you can't go wrong with any of the shakes that Honey Butter blends up.

5. Chicken Shawarma pita-Jaffa Middle Eastern Kitchen, El Jebel

The baked goods at Jaffa Middle Eastern Kitchen are like a little slice of heaven, but given the namesake, there is also a great selection of Middle Eastern food that can transport you there with just a few bites, such as their chicken shawarma pita.

The sandwich features slow-roasted chicken marinated in herbs and oil, an Israeli-style salad, and tahini all wrapped up in soft, warm pita bread that can get a bit messy but is worth grabbing a few extra napkins to enjoy.

6. House Potatoes-Capitol Creek Brewery, El Jebel

Yes, I am putting potatoes on a list of the best foods in the valley, but once you taste the incredible house potatoes offered at Capitol Creek Brewery, you will see why.

These potatoes are done in the style of classic smashed fried potatoes, that's where you crush par-boiled small potatoes before frying them, resulting in potatoes that are ultra-crispy on the outside and fluffy on the inside, these are potatoes that you might as well have as your entrée.

7. Trout Dip-The Tipsy Trout, Basalt

This is a bit of a personal suggestion because The Tipsy Trout happens to be where I used to work before I decided to become a writer…I would prefer not to go into details as to why.

While there is a good deal of food to try, one item that people in the valley can't seem to get enough of is their smoked trout dip, flavored with things like honey, jalapeno, and cream cheese, then served with warm pita bread and some pickled jalapenos for a smoky, sweet, slightly spicy bite.

8. Smoked Half Chicken-Home Team BBQ, Buttermilk

Any good barbecue place should know how to do proper chicken, but at Home Team BBQ, located near the Aspen airport, they seem to know how to make it great by getting the chicken's skin incredibly crispy while maintaining that great smoke flavor that all barbecued meat must have and while keeping the chicken itself so juicy that you can practically forget the sauce.

9. Salsa Verde Nachos-Woody Creek Tavern, near Aspen Airport

Nachos are a true American favorite, there's just something about those piles of tortilla chips smothered with gooey, melty cheese that can make anyone's mouth water, and the salsa verde nachos over at Woody Creek Tavern hit all those comforting notes and more.

Nutty Mexican cheese blend, plump black bean salsa, and tangy Salsa Verde all piled up on those chips for a messy but delicious bite that I know you will love.

Although, unless you're a vegetarian, I strongly suggest adding their tender, juicy carne asada to your nachos, you'll thank me later.

10. The Italian Job pizza-Mezzaluna, El Jebel and Aspen

I've already stated my love of Italian food; I practically have marinara sauce for blood and parmesan cheese for muscles at this point, so you can believe me when I say that the Italian job pizza over at Mezzaluna (Italian word for half-moon) is worth every penny and every calorie.

Featuring nduja (a type of spicy sausage), salty mortadella, and gooey mozzarella cheese, all sitting on top of their crisp, house-made pizza crust that is cooked in a brick oven, I can guarantee that this might become your new favorite pizza.

TOP 10 SOUVENIRS TO GET IN THE ROARING FORK VALLEY

1. Locally made jams.

It seems a bit cliché, but stands at farmer's markets in the valley do provide some incredible jams made from locally grown fruit such as peaches, plums, or apricots that, with proper storage, can stick around for quite some time. I suppose you could also attempt to smuggle the fresh versions of those fruits, but they likely won't last nearly as long.

You can always ask the vendors for a taste of each jam to ensure it has the flavor profile you're looking for, and it's a great way to support local businesses.

2. Woody Creek Distillers whiskey

Yes, sir, here is my third time mentioning Woody Creek Distillers, but given that it is a locally owned company in the valley that produces some of the finest spirits the valley has to offer, there's no reason why I shouldn't, as they do make great gifts, especially for those liquor experts who can taste all sorts of subtle flavors with one sip.

While flying with bottles of whiskey or gin in your suitcase does pose some risks, it is worth it to bring the taste of the Roaring Fork Valley to your home.

3. **Locally made jewelry**.

Mountains are full of rocks...I suppose that isn't a surprise, but with that comes some amazing gemstones that can be refined into some of the most stunning and incredible jewelry the Rocky Mountains has to offer. If you're looking to make your loved ones feel special, then the locally-made jewelry found in farmer's markets and in select valley shops is what the doctor called for.

4. **Welcome to Colorful Colorado sign ornament.**

Christmas tree ornaments might seem like another one of those cliché souvenirs, but I do think they're a great reminder of places that you've been, where your loved ones are from, and of some of the fond memories that you create in those places.

While there are many kinds of ornaments that can be found in souvenir shops all over the valley, one that I found quite charming is a small wooden ornament that is designed like the *Welcome to Colorful Colorado* sign, as Colorado is a place for great memories and happy thoughts.

5. Locally made paintings.

They say a picture is worth a thousand words, but the paintings that RFV artists draw up might as well be worth millions as each one does its job in capturing the natural beauty that makes up the Colorado mountains as if that were possible.

Like with the jewelry, these paintings can be found in farmer's markets, in Aspen, there is a weekly outdoor art gallery that runs on Thursdays during the summer months, and there are plenty of art shops studded throughout the RFV towns that will likely have the next piece for your personal gallery.

6. Freeze Dried candy and fruit.

While I don't entirely understand the process of freeze-drying and how it works, I can certainly appreciate the results when brought to me from a vendor that pops up in Carbondale farmer's markets whose freeze-dried products are crunchy, airy perfection.

My recommendations would be the freeze-dried peaches, as the freeze-drying process seems to enhance their tartness, and, if you're feeling brave, some freeze-dried ice cream sandwiches that have the flavor of an Oreo cookie with lots of crunchy goodness.

7. A luxury piece from The Little Nell gift shop.

The Little Nell is one of the most luxurious hotels in Aspen, and their gift shop, conveniently located in the lobby, is full of items that any lover of luxury would go nuts for.

With items like dog treats and pre-packaged food from Element 47, The Little Nell's in-house restaurant, you are guaranteed to give you the feel of luxury in your own home. They also have online shopping, so you don't even need to be a guest at The Little Nell to get some of their gift shop items.

8. Aspen Monopoly

If you're a board game lover, specifically a Monopoly lover, then the Aspen-themed game is exactly what you need.

77

As one would expect, Aspen Monopoly follows the classic rules of the money-based game but gives it a unique twist with iconic locations in or near Aspen and is sure to bring a bit of Aspen fun to your own home, wherever that might be. As you might expect, the game also has some cute mountain-themed game pieces, such as a gondola car, a bear, and an Aspen leaf, so it'll feel like you're walking through the entire Aspen Mountain region without ever leaving your home.

9. A cute stuffed animal

Yes, it is another cliché souvenir, but considering all of the roaming animals that are found in the Roaring Fork Valley, you would be a fool not to take one or two stuffed critters home with you, especially if you have or need a gift for kids.

Perhaps you want a fluffy grizzly bear to watch over the fish you have in your home, or a powerful bighorn sheep to give your kids a sense of protection, or would like to have a cute chipmunk that you'll have to fight to keep away from the nuts, any stuffed animal you pick up in RFV will definitely be a great gift for those that you love.

10. Cannabis chocolates

Alright, I'm aware that one of the reasons why some people venture up to Colorado is because of the local cannabis dispensaries. While I don't partake in that particular activity, I do think that if you are going to do anything weed-related, having a way to take some home with you would not be a bad idea, such as the cannabis chocolates found in certain shops in the valley.

TOP 10 MUST TAKE PICTURES IN THE ROARING FORK VALLEY

1. Mt. Sopris

One of the largest mountains you can spot in the valley, Mt. Sopris looms over Carbondale like a high-flying eagle and can be a fantastic photo opportunity for your whole family. The best place to get a photo of Sopris would have to be at a viewing point near the North end of Carbondale, and you'd be extra lucky if you could get the photo while Sopris still has a bit of snow left on it in the spring.

2. **Fall foliage near Aspen**.

If there is one tourist attraction that keeps people coming back to Aspen year after year in the fall, it has to be the incredible foliage that lines the beautiful trees found all over Aspen and the valley.

Giving you all the colors of red, orange, yellow, and a bit of green, the foliage in Aspen feels like something right out of a painting. While there is hardly a bad spot to get a photo of those colorful leaves, one of my go-to spots is the mountain road between Basalt and the turn-off to Snowmass along Highway 82.

3. The Roaring Fork River

There is but one river that runs through and essentially carved out what the Roaring Fork Valley is today, and that is the stunning Roaring Fork River that happens to run right behind my house in Glenwood Springs.

Running from Independence Lake, at an elevation of about 12,500 feet, all the way through the valley and eventually connecting with the Colorado River in Glenwood, I do not know what the valley would look like if it weren't for this stunning, trout-filled river.

The cool part is that anywhere you go along Highway 82, you will likely find a great spot to take a photo or several of the river and its natural glory; plus, there are several side areas along the highway that you can stop in to get photos as well.

4. Wild elk herds

Elk is a bit of a Colorado/Rocky Mountain specialty, and just about any time of the year you can find vast herds of these massive deer that stud the open fields in the valley, it is truly a sight to behold.

However, if you are lucky enough to spot one of these herds, then I strongly recommend that you proceed with caution and take those photos of the elk from afar. The average adult male elk can weigh between 710 and 730 pounds, and that's not even getting into the powerful antlers they pack, so it is best to let the elk mind their business, and they will likely mind yours.

5. Top of Mushroom Rock near Carbondale

I already mentioned the incredible Mushroom Rock hiking trail, but I do realize that not everyone has the energy for a 1.5-mile hike, but fortunately, the trail also has a stunning view that only requires a 15-20 minute, easy hike, and that would be at the top of Mushroom Rock.

With this view, you get an overlook at the entire town of Carbondale to get a sense of how large this small mountain town really is, and if you're lucky you might also see a few birds fly over and do a few little flips or loops in the air. Given the slightly uphill path, you can imagine that the hike up Mushroom Rock can get a bit muddy and slick, especially after rainfall, so be mindful of the weather if you plan on heading over there.

6. Back of Sunlight Mountain.

While Sunlight Mountain near Glenwood Springs has its fair share of ski trails for a good amount of winter fun, there is one other advantage to paying a visit to the incredible mountain, and that is the stunning view that can only be seen from the back end of Sunlight; a view that pictures can't possibly do justice, but it's certainly nice to try.

To get to this view, you will need to take the short Segundo lift, then ski down to the left over to the Primo lift, which will take you up Sunlight's peak where you will dismount and ski around a corner off to the left from where you get off.

The result: An incredible view of several stunning mountains near the area, including Mt. Sopris, and a view that might get you to forget skiing all together and stare at it all day.

7. Maroon Lake

Again, let's say you wish to visit the Maroon Bells over in Highlands but don't wish to take the rocky

3.5-mile hike over to Crater Lake, what you could consider is the mile-long but easier hike over to Maroon Lake and get blown away by the crystal-clear water that makes for another excellent photo-op.

Once up there, you might also want to consider the 3-mile walk around the circumference of the lake to get even more views and great chances to take photos.

8. The top of Independence Pass

As stated, the winding road along Independence Pass has no shortage of stunning views, but there are not many great places to pull over and take pictures, which is why it's a good thing that at the very top of the pass lies the highest drivable point in the valley.

Sitting on top of the Continental Divide, named so because it is a mountainous region that practically divides North America, the peak of Independence Pass features a view that stretches for dozens of miles in almost every direction and has just as many ideal places to take pictures.

9. Top of Aspen's Silver Queen Gondola

Going a bit down but still maintaining a very high altitude, Aspen's Silver Queen Gondola is a 15 minute ride from bottom to top, but once you get up there, you can appreciate the stunning views that can only be seen from the top of Aspen Mountain.

It doesn't matter if you're heading up there in the summer, winter, or in between, the top of the Silver Queen Gondola is the place to go if you're looking to take stunning pictures and possibly have a bit of mountain peak fun as, in the summer, there are some games and attractions set up.

The only real downside is that a trip up the gondola costs about $20 per person, but I guarantee that the sights are worth the price.

10. The Fairy Caves

Sitting at the peak of the Glenwood Gondola lies two stunning cave systems that are well worth spotting if you find yourself in Glenwood Springs.

The Fairy Caves, given their name from a stalagmite that has a resemblance to a Chinese goddess, offers a wide range of cave rock formations like stalagmites and stalactites that makes it feel like stepping into a new world, and it is worth getting some photos of those formations.

While you're up there, you might as well get some snaps that overview the entire town of Glenwood

Springs and get a strong clue as to why I've been living in that little town for years.

TOP 10 SITES TO SEE IN THE ROARING FORK VALLEY

1. Hayes Creek Falls

I briefly mentioned these incredible falls in my section about the Beaver Lake located next to Marble, about 30 miles South of Carbondale, but I feel like it would be nice to dive deeper into what makes the Hayes Creek Falls such an incredible sight to see.

Sitting on the edge of the gorgeous Highway 133 is a set of waterfalls that are easy to walk to from the road, is stunning to look at, and, if you get close enough, almost drowns out all sounds so you can ease your mind, even just for a few moments. If you're looking to hop around the valley and see some of the best sights, then the Hayes Creek Falls should be on your list.

2. Aspen Mountain

I likely don't need to tell you that Aspen Mountain, or any of the four ski mountains in the area, is a sight to behold, stretching up to 11,212 feet with all sorts of trees, bushes, and the occasional chipmunk.

87

Seeing Aspen Mountain up close is nice, but right after a winding mountainous part of Highway 82, you can get a full view of the mountain, as well as Buttermilk Mountain and Highlands Mountain, from afar, giving you a sense of how mighty the mountains of Aspen are.

3. Street Art

Something you might not expect to find in the little RFV towns is a wide array of street art and sculptures that add character to those cities and show what sort of minds make up the valley. As much as I would love to tell you about each and every piece of art that can be found in the valley…that will have to be for another book, so here are a few examples of this art that you can find in Glenwood Springs.

The running horses painting under the 7th street bridge, several butterfly wings that line the walls of some of the downtown Glenwood buildings, and even near my house, you can find an electric box that has a painting of a chipmunk among several aspen trees, and that's just a taste of the dozens of other artwork found in Glenwood and the other RFV towns.

4. Sayre Park

One of the many perks of living in Glenwood Springs is that it's a small town, so just about everything I could possibly need is within a 5-10 minute drive from my house, and sitting within that distance is a stunning park that Glenwood residents go into like swarms of bees: Sayre Park.

From the moment you step into this gorgeous park, located in Hyland Park Avenue off Grand Avenue, you are instantly drawn in by the natural beauty of cooling trees, flowers, and a huge football field that my little dog, Ziggy, absolutely loves running through.

Also, since the park is right next to an Elementary school, the students head over to that park for recess almost every day…as long as it's still warm.

5. Ruedi Reservoir

Like with Hayes Creek Falls, I don't know if this is technically in the valley, but it is a massive body of water that is certainly worth taking a drive to: Ruedi Reservoir.

Located about 15 miles East of Basalt, the Ruedi Reservoir, as well as the Ruedi Dam (built from 1964-1968), sits in the White River National Forest and stores approximately 102,00-acre feet of water that feeds into the Frying Pan River, which meets up with the Roaring Fork River in Basalt.

If you ever get the chance, take the drive over to the Ruedi Reservoir and take a good, long look at the massive amount of water that it contains, maybe spot a few boaters or fisherman while you're at it.

6. Bethel Plaza, under the 7th Street bridge in Glenwood Springs.

To me, one of the most precious hidden gems Glenwood Springs has to offer is the cool and charming Bethel Plaza under the Grand Avenue Bridge that connects Northern Glenwood to Downtown.

An area that was updated in recent years to go from underutilized space to a place for social interactions and the occasional live music, Bethel Plaza, named after Executive of Glenwood's Downtown Development Authority (DDA), Leslie Bethel, connects several restaurants in the Downtown Glenwood area and even gives open seating to anyone wishing to hang out and relax under the big bridge.

Bethel Plaza is also where the Glenwood Farmer's Market is held every Tuesday during the summertime.

7.   Snow-Covered Plains

If there is one thing that lights up the Roaring Fork Valley during the wintertime, it is the abundant snow that covers the whole valley like a thick blanket, and while the snow-covered mountains are something to behold, I always find myself fascinated at the wide plains when they are snow draped.

This sort of thing is especially noticeable in the areas between Glenwood, Carbondale, and El Jebel, as when the sun comes out and glistens over the white powder, it causes the entire area to glow in a stunning way.

Of course, if you wish to come up to the valley to see the incredible snow-covered mountains of Aspen or Snowmass, then that's fine too.

8.   Doc Holiday Memorial

A legend of the American West, John Henry (Doc) Holiday, who died of tuberculosis in November of 1887, happens to be buried at the Limewood Cemetery in Glenwood Springs, located at the end of 12th Street.

After going through a short but moderately challenging hiking trail, you will come across the historic gravesite and be able to take in a bit of Glenwood Springs history.

History buffs and outdoors lovers will most likely enjoy the trail and the experience of seeing the final resting place for the American gambler, gunfighter, and dentist.

9.   Aspen 4th of July Parade.

The 4th of July is already a day for patriotic celebration, parades, and as much cold beer as the country can handle, but if you ever find yourself in or near Aspen on America's holiday, then you have got to check out the incredible street parade held every year.

For the parade, all of Aspen's Main Street is closed in order for dozens of floats, musicians, and cars can walk on through to show the valley how they celebrate patriotic pride, and you can bet that there's also plenty of food, drinks, and souvenirs to go around.

Now, if you are already planning on checking out the incredible parade, then I strongly suggest leaving your car/rental car behind and taking the RFTA bus over into Aspen as the crowds tend to be jam packed, and if you're willing to stick around a few more hours, then there's also a stunning firework display to end the day right.

10. Snowmass Alpine Coaster

While there is no shortage of winter fun over in Aspen Snowmass, there is one attraction that doesn't involve skiing but can still get you to feel the cool wind in your hair and take in the glory of the forest, and that is the Snowmass Alpine Coaster.

Located at the top of the Elk Camp Gondola, The Alpine Coaster features several turns and drops on a metal track for about 20 minutes of fun. In addition, you get to decide how fast you go down the coaster as there are two levers on the side of the single car that you sit in that you push down to go as fast or as slow as you wish.

TOP 10 CULTURE SHOCKS WHEN VISITING THE ROARING FORK VALLEY

1. Dry, high-altitude climate.

It is a simple fact that living in the mountains means getting a bit higher above sea level than you would otherwise, even over in Mile-high Denver, you can still feel the effects.

Altitude sickness, chapped lips, and getting dehydrated quicker are all common issues that people can experience, especially if you've never been to the mountains before, even someone like me who has lived in the valley for more than five years sometimes still feels the effects of the altitude, especially whenever I go skiing or hiking.

My biggest tips to help avoid these are simple: Drink lots of water or other fluids (if you find yourself going to the bathroom more frequently, you're doing it right), take it easy if you need to, and if it helps then consider taking altitude sickness medication before you venture up to the Rockies.

2. How quickly you can feel intoxicated while drinking.

I mentioned this early on, but being at high altitude means many things, one of those being that alcohol can go through your system at a faster rate, so you can find yourself feeling intoxicated much faster than places at sea level.

The reason for this is that the lower air pressure and lower oxygen levels cause the body to absorb alcohol at a faster rate than at sea level, and while you don't necessarily get drunk faster, your body does process the alcohol faster, so you feel the effects of being drunk quicker.

Drink responsibly, have a designated driver around, if possible, and be mindful of the fact if you decide to hit up the local Roaring Fork Valley bars.

3. How wide open the scenery is.

When some people think of mountain life, you likely think of winding roads, tight spaces, and countless mountains from left and right, but what they might not realize is that there is a lot of open space in the Roaring Fork Valley, especially once you get outside of the valley towns.

While there are definitely a lot of mountains to go around, between those mountains lies a charming, open atmosphere that many farmers and ranchers take advantage of to give the local produce and goods that we need.

4. "If you hate the weather in the Roaring Fork Valley, just wait five minutes."

I think it's established that mountain weather can be like a bipolar person who refuses to take their medications (no offense to anyone), and just one week of staying in the valley can show you just that.

I have seen it go from clear skies to cloudy to pouring rain in a matter of minutes, and that's not even covering some of the intense blizzards and lightning storms that we get from time to time. If you're an indoors lover like me, then this shouldn't be much of a problem, but if outdoor fun calls you, then…I wish you the best of luck.

5. How many bikers, skiers, and rafters/kayakers there are.

It seems like in just about every home in the Roaring Fork Valley, you will find at least one kayak, pair of skis, mountain bike, or any other sort of athletic equipment that all look like they've gotten some use in recent years, and there's no reason they shouldn't.

All over the valley, you will find a diverse range of hiking trails, ski trails, and rivers that call outdoor lovers and athletes like the loudest megaphone, and all of which deliver their own version of fun to be had.

6. Cultural Diversity for the Restaurants

To me, one of the best parts about living in the Roaring Fork Valley is seeing how diverse of a landscape and population there is, as everywhere you go, you will see all sorts of different people with different backgrounds, beliefs, and cultures that come together to form the great melting pot that is this great valley.

This diversity is also very apparent with the food, like some of the restaurants in Glenwood Springs for example, we have Indian, Mexican, Japanese, and so much more, it's like you can travel the entire world without ever leaving the valley.

And that's just here in Glenwood, there's also Middle Eastern food in El Jebel, German food in Aspen, Thai food in Carbondale, the list goes on and on, and I believe it is one of the many things that make this valley the perfect place to call home.

7.   Road Danger

Mountain roads can be dangerous, especially during the winter when the snow freezes up at night and turns into ice, and that's not even diving into the chance of rockslides, floods, or drunk drivers due to the faster rate of feeling drunk.

Unless you have experience with driving on snow/ice and have a car that you trust is able to go on terrains like that, then I would suggest giving the RFTA bus line a shot for winter transportation.

As for the summer, while the risks do go down somewhat, the winding roads between Basalt and Aspen can be a bit of a hazard if you're not careful enough, so ease your foot off the gas pedal and keep a sharp eye out for anything hazardous that might be on the road.

8. Jam Packed Weekends

During the weekends, holidays, and especially during the summertime, it seems like most Colorado residents, including those in the Roaring Fork Valley, want to venture up to the mountains for a bit of rafting, skiing, or any other kind of mountain fun, leading to crowds so large that there's almost no wiggle room.

This is especially true for restaurants, I speak from personal experience, and tourist attractions like the Glenwood Adventure Park or the ski mountains as they seem to have the logic of 'if that's where everyone else is going, then I'm going there too.', it can make mountain traveling a bit of a hassle.

9. Vast Nature

If there is one fact that is true no matter who you talk to, it's that the Roaring Fork Valley is full of some of the most stunning and breathtaking views of nature that make the valley feel like it is its own separate world from the bustling city of Denver.

The list of incredible natural sights to see in the valley goes on and on, from the sky-high Mount Sopris to the roaring rivers to the dense, wildlife-filled forests.

Personally, one of my favorite natural sights to see happens to be the sight I look at every time I sit on my computer to write up the content I make, that being the incredible mountains of Glenwood Springs.

10. Lack of Clubbing

While I do not partake, I do understand that, in many cities, people will spend their free time going out to some club or adult bar for some drinks and dancing; however, in the Roaring Fork Valley, that sort of clubbing is almost nonexistent.

It could have to do with the smaller-town vibes or the fact that many locals don't have as much free time on their hands as they wish, but it seems like you don't hear anyone talking about 'hitting the club'.

However, where the valley lacks clubs, we more than make up for breweries where groups of people gather up for some tasty beer and some fun.

10 SCAMS I SHOULD LOOK OUT FOR WHEN VISITING THE ROARING FORK VALLEY

1. Towel Charge

Not sure if it counts as a scam, but if you're going to one of the hot springs in Glenwood, make sure you bring your own towel as they do charge extra for towels.

Most of the hotels/motels in the valley have plenty of towels to go around, so I'm sure they wouldn't mind you bringing a few to the hot springs as long as you make sure to return them at the end of the day.

2. Ka-Ching

It's well-established that Aspen is an expensive town, and as a result, there are a good handful of restaurants and shops that will attempt to overcharge you for food and other goods. While I can't say for certain which shops do this, I would advise looking around at multiple shops to see how their prices match up.

Taxi Driver's Bonus

As it is with many tourists or travelers, taxi or Uber drivers will try to take a "scenic" drive that ends up costing you way more money than the trip should be worth, so keep a map handy. In fact, I would forget about taxis all altogether and take the RFTA bus, if I need to get from one of the valley's towns to the other, plus most shops or restaurants are located within walking distance from the hotels.

3. Rental Headache

Let's say you wish to rent a mountain bike to do some extra exploring of the valley on your own, but when the day comes, and you go to return the bike, the owner tries to charge you extra for 'damages' that weren't your fault. While a mountain bike is certainly meant for outdoors, paying for damages that weren't your fault can be a hassle.

My advice is to take several photos of the bike(s) soon after you get them, so you can show the shop owner that the bike is still in the same relative shape it was in when it was rented out, the same can be said for ski equipment and kayaks.

4. Shady Smokes

While marijuana is legal in the state of Colorado, you definitely need to be careful about where you're getting your cannabis fix from. While I do not smoke it, myself, if I did, then my best bet would be to get weed from a reputable cannabis shop such as Green Dragon, who know how to sell their herb safely and legally for the valley to enjoy.

5. Flight Risk

While the airport in Aspen might seem convenient as it's right in the mountains, you do end up paying extra for a small layover that, especially in the winter, could end up waiting for your connecting flight much longer than expected.

I suggest flying into the Denver airport and then either renting a car or taking the Amtrak that runs through Glenwood up to the mountains.

6. Non-official Tickets

This also feels like general travel advice, but if someone off the streets comes up to you at a bus station or even in the ski areas and claims they can sell you bus passes/ski lift tickets for X amount of money, it's most likely a big scam to get access to your credit card info. Always buy tickets from official websites (See Other Resources) or ticket booths.

7. Nitpicking Officers

Given the winding roads of the valley and the sort of weather it can experience, especially in the wintertime, there are always one or two police officers lurking around trying to find people who are speeding or showing reckless driving behavior. I, unfortunately, have found myself in similar situations, none of which have led to me getting a ticket of any sort, thank goodness, but still.   The way to avoid this is simple: drive safely, use public transportation if there's harsh weather, and keep an eye on that speedometer.

8. Auto-Gratuity

This is also a general tip when it comes to dining, but sometimes, when you're at a restaurant and have already paid the check, you might see a tab on the bottom that reads 'suggested gratuity,' which can be a scam. While I can't speak for all restaurants, there are a few who use this to get you to pay more money for your tip than you might expect.

Your best bet would be to calculate the percentages yourself, as restaurants often tempt you into tipping more than the percentage is.

9. Bang for your Bowl

Sometimes, when you're skiing, you'll want to stop by some of the on-mountain restaurants for a quick bite of food before getting back out to the slopes, and soup is certainly a great way to warm you up on those cold winter days, however there are places who will attempt to give you less soup for a fixed price.

Of course, you can always ask the workers to fill your soup bowl up a bit more, but it is something to watch out for.

OTHER RESOURCES:

- RFTA mobile app for purchasing bus passes, looking up the bus timetable, and tracking when the next bus arrives.
- Wanderlust.com: If you're in Glenwood but wish to board your furry friend so you can have a bit of extra RFV fun, then Wanderlust Doggie Daycare Center is just what you need. (970) 366-4426
- Fodors.com: guide for traveling Aspen and the valley.
- Aspenchamber.com: With everything you need to know about traveling to Aspen.
- Visitglenwood.com: With everything you need to know about traveling to Glenwood Springs.
- Sunlightmtn.com: where you can apply for lift passes and see how the slopes are day by day.
- Aspensnowmass.com: Where you can order lift passes for the Aspen Mountains.
- COtrip.org: for information about traveling in Colorado.
- The Aspen Snowmass App-to keep up to date with Aspen news, weather, and more.
- Pastalove.net: Italian food blog by Scotty Jeffus…who lives in the valley.

TASTE OF THE SEASONS

Bethel Plaza Farmer's Market
Held every Tuesday from Mid-June to September under the 7th Street bridge in Glenwood Springs

Carbondale Farmer's Market
Held every Wednesday during that same time at Sopris Park

Basalt Sunday Market
Held every Sunday at Ponderosa Park

Strawberry Days Festival
Two Rivers Park in Glenwood Springs held the weekend of or around June 21st.

The Kristie Ennis Foundation (TKEF) Oktoberfest
The second week of October at Sunlight Mountain Resort

Heritage Fire Food Festival
Held late July at the Aspen Snowmass Base Village

Winter X Games
Last weekend of January in Buttermilk

Aspen Gay Ski Week
Mid-January in the Aspen ski Mountains (check dates online)

107

READ OTHER BOOKS BY CZYK PUBLISHING

CZYKPublishing.com